Mr. Max

by Lisa Robinson • illustrated by Kimberley Barnes

I am Mr. Max.

I zip up and go.

I go to my job.

My job is here!

I see a big, big log.

Can I fix it? Yes!

I have an ax.

I can cut the big log.

Six foxes have a den.

I can see the foxes.

The little foxes zig zag, zig zag.

I sit on a box.

I like my job a lot!